The Magical Tree 2

Powers & Presences

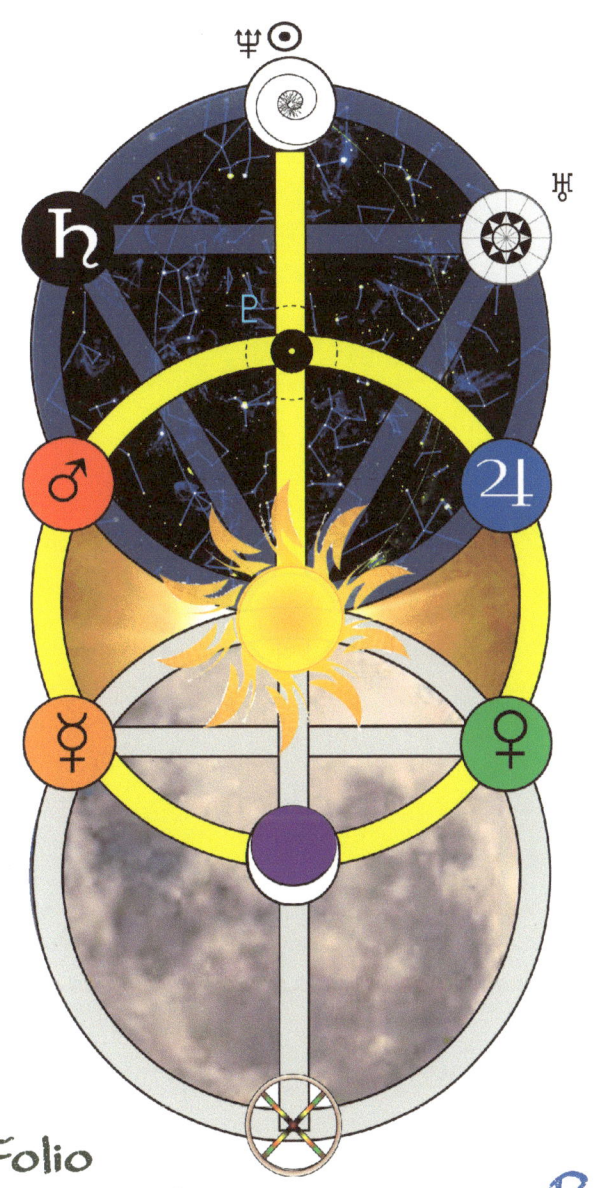

A Green Fire Folio

By
Coleston Brown

Copyright ©2008-2013 Coleston Brown

All rights reserved. No part of this book may be reproduced or transmitted in any form without written permission from the author except for the inclusion of brief quotations in a review.

ISBN-13: 978-0986591280

Published in 2013 by

Le Brun Publications

Canada, Ireland

Cover art and design

by Coleston Brown

Book design by Coleston Brown

A Green Fire Folio on the Magical Way

Contents

Author's Note and Acknowledgments ... 4
Part I: Enabling the Magical Tree: The Ten Powers and the Void ... 5
The Tenth Power: The Power of Expression. ... 6
The Ninth Power: Foundational Power; Sexual Energies. ... 7
The Eighth Power: The Power of Pattern Making, Thinking, Intellect. ... 8
The Seventh Power: The Power of Emotion, Attraction, Attainment. ... 9
The Sixth Power: The Mediating Power, Harmony, Interchanging Radiant Energies, Healing. ... 10
The Fifth Power: The Power that Removes, Catabolic Energy, Taking, Discipline ... 11
The Fourth Power: The Power that Bestows, Anabolic Energy, Giving, Compassion. ... 12
The Third Power: Universal Enfolding Power; Inflowing, Enveloping Energies; First Forms ... 13
Second Power: Universal Outflowing Power, Outgoing Creative Energy, Wisdom ... 14
The First Power: The Source, The Summit, Origination. ... 15
The Power of No-Thing: The Void, the Stillness, the Mystery. ... 16
Notes to Part I ... 17
Practicing the Powers I: Raising the Powers ... 18
Part II: Enlivening The Magical Tree— The Mystery & The Ten Presences ... 21
0 & 1 The Mystery & The Source ... 22
2 The High One, The Utterer. ... 23
3 The Deep One, The Enfolder ... 24
4 The Sovereign, Benefactor or Giving Presence ... 25
5 The Warrior or Taking Presence ... 26
6 The Radiant One ... 27
7 The Lover ... 28
8 The Knower, The Mentor, The Smith ... 29
9 The Weaver/Upholder ... 30
10 The Illuminated Landscape, The Dreamer ... 31
Relational Polarity and The Presences ... 32
Working with Presences: ... 33
Practicing the Presences I The Empty Chair: ... 33
Practicing the Presences II The Wheel of Presences: ... 33
About The Author ... 34
Picture Credits ... 34

Author's Note and Acknowledgments

This Folio deals with the all-important subjects of Primal Powers and Presences on the Magical Tree. Here you will discover insights that are useful for anyone who studies and works with the Magical Tree, whether this be with the archaic forms assimilated to the shamanic pole (cosmic axis), drum and Tree Goddess, or with the philosophical, mystical and occultic incarnations of Qabalah.* And yet, while the material given here illuminates these other approaches to the Tree, it is not specific to those forms. The Magical Tree incorporates universal forms, patterns, and energies that have been retained through the ages in later and different forms of the Tree.

These writings present the Magical Tree as a practical tradition rooted in the great lunar, solar and stellar cycles in which our ancestors participated and from which they drew deep understanding, awareness, and harmony of being.

Thanks are due to all those with whom I have discussed the material presented here, including those spiritual presences with whom I live each day. Heart-felt thanks to Faery Artist Jessie Skillen, for much support, encouragement and helpful conversation, as well as useful advice on the content and design of this Folio. Special thanks to Cliff and Pauline McClinton, and also to "Twilight and "the Pixie" for ongoing support and encouragement.

Regarding the Images in this Folio: For Part I, on the Powers, I have chosen appropriate images from nature to represent the Primal powers of the Tree, while Part II, which deals with the Presences, is illustrated equally appropriately by images from the work of the visionary poet and painter, William Blake (1757-1827). Scholars have long been aware of connections between the work of William Blake and the Magical Tree in Qabalistc Tradition.§

Coleston Brown —Carrowreagh, County Sligo, Éire, 2013.

---

* To paraphrase what I have written elsewhere regarding my choice of spelling for this word: The English letters QBL share the same predecessors as their Hebrew counterparts. The modern conventional spelling "Kabbalah" now in common usage seems to have arisen as an effort by modern academics, to supplant the more esoterically accurate rendering of the word with one that is, at best, a pandering to Philology and phonetics ,and at worst, an attempt to alter the energetic meaning of the tradition itself.

§ For a recent treatment see in particular Sheila Spector's ***Wonders Divine: The Development of Blake's Kabbalistic Myth*** and ***Glorious Incomprehensible: The Development of Blake's Kabbalistic Language***. both published by Brucknell University Press, Lewisburg: 2001.

Part I: *Enabling the Magical Tree:*
The Ten Powers and the Void

In the pattern of the Magical Tree there are Ten[1] Primal Powers that flow from the stillness of the Void. The Powers are resonant with the seven star forms (Sun, Moon and planets/wandering stars), which were considered in Folio 1. But whereas the star forms express and embody the primal lore and archaic experience of the Tree, the Powers enable the Magical Tree.

The word "power" means to be able. To be empowered is to be enabled. The teachings of the Magical Tree speak of the Powers that flow between Wheels, Worlds, Realms, and Beings. These spiritual or magical powers permeate reality and flow in and out of life situations. Contact with these universal energies (which cannot be controlled, only mediated) is transformative and authentically empowering.

The Ten Powers are not the Spheres of the Tree, for the Spheres are broad fields of influence, holisms, that exceed the commingling or summation of individual forces within them. The Powers are, however, the central, core energies around which the influences of the Spheres interweave. The Powers are Universal energies that course through all Realms, Worlds, and beings. These energies permeate our reality and flow in and out of life situations. Conscious contact with the Powers (which cannot be controlled, only mediated) is transformative and enabling.

The Powers of the Magical Tree can be approached from a variety of perspectives. One of these, the Lightning flash or Zag, can be followed in descending or ascending fashion. It will be useful here to follow the Powers in ascending fashion from Tenth to First. Like physical lightning, the Lightning Zag on the Tree strikes from both directions – above and below. Physical lightning actually consists of a double zigzag–two strokes: a leader that zigzags from the sky to the ground, and a return strike that flashes up the

The Lightning Zag on the Magical Tree.

path made by the leader. This theme or cycle of ascent or descent and return is a dynamic encountered often in inner work based on the structure of the Magical Tree.

The Tenth Power:
The Power of Expression.

Although there are myriad forms and modes of expressing Being, one of the most ancient and enduring patterns is that of the Elements.[2] In the West, these are four — Air, Fire, Water & Earth. *Being* or *Spirit* (which is sometimes misrepresented as a "Fifth Element") is the energy that enlivens and unifies the Elements.

That the Four Elements articulate Being is remarkably evident in our own vocabulary. Words such as airy, flighty, earthy, fiery, watery and stormy, show how integral the Elements are to human identity. The Elements, because they express Being, unite all beings. Thus humans, animals, insects, plants, fey, nature spirits and all the rest have in common their fourfold elemental nature, their elemental expression of Being.[3]

There is what might be called the Elemental Way of magical/spiritual development, which attempts to balance the personality by harmonising the Elements. Although apparently simplistic, the Elemental Way is capable of considerable sophistication. However, it is a practical method more than a system of analysis or categorisation. Work with the Elements is a primal way of healing and empowerment — a fact rediscovered in some forms of modern psychology where the Elements appear thinly disguised as four psychological functions. Unfortunately, this kind of approach lifts an age-old awareness and understanding of Being out of its original magical context and forces it into the somewhat narrow framework of psychology. The significance of the Elemental Way, however, extends far beyond the therapist's or theorist's purview, for it deals with the expression of the essence of Life in the Universe. Of course, this is a qualitative understanding, not a quantitative formula such as permeates much of modernist thought. The Elemental Way is about acknowledging and relating to reality in terms of the expressive characteristics of valued beings, not the grotesque reduction of life to a series of formulas, measurements and calculations.[4]

It could be said that the Tenth Power expresses and realises the other nine Powers, which flow into the manifest world through elemental forms.

The 10th Power is the embodiment and expression of the Four Elements as the ground of reality, in both the physical and spiritual sense.

At left: The Four Elements centred on Spirit.

The Ninth Power:
Foundational Power; Sexual Energies.

The Foundational Power or Life Energy is above all a rhythmic power: it undulates, cycles and spirals; it whirls and turns and rises and falls. In ancient times the vital force was seen to ascend from the deep earth or descend from the stars into living things via the primal fluids of water, blood and semen. The Foundational Power is thus intimately linked to sexual energies, which in broadest terms are the energies of life, death, and interchange.

A lot of purported sex magic or polarity work is merely an attempt to escape from unfulfilling personal experiences and relationships by redirecting the sexual energies into romanticised magical partnerships. Such false idealisations are often buttressed by self-inflating methods of mutual infatuation or "flattery magic" (all under the guise of assuming "god forms"). This is the sad and unhealthy legacy of closed and repressive occult fraternities of an earlier age, whose defunct and dated methods still influence many contemporary students of magic.

The problem extends not only to assumed magical partnerships among living humans, but also to similar relationships with inner or spiritual beings. Relationships with Sacred Presences and spiritual beings generally follow patterns that duplicate, or compensate for, the nature and quality of our outer world relationships, and vice versa. In any case, wholesome, healthy relationships, physically sexual and otherwise, go a long way towards making the bulk of so-called polarity work unnecessary and irrelevant.

Few realise that human sexual energy is itself closely tied to the earth and stars through the daily rhythms and fluctuations of light and energy around and through the planet. Part of magical training is to learn to link the human body to deep power centres in the landscape, under-earth and stars. This is known as the arousal of the Faery Fire or dragon power, and extends into the mystery of the awakening or rousing of Primal Beings that slumber in the stars and earth.

River deltas are places of fertility and rhythm. Their triangular shape supports their feminine symbolism and enhances their significance as embodiments of the Vulva of the Goddess who may be associated with the land and whose womb is the sea. *Above*: the Volga River Delta. *Inset*: the Venus of Laussel, ca 25,000 BCE.

The Eighth Power:
The Power of Pattern Making, Thinking, Intellect.

Pattern making is an important power for the magical practitioner. The ability to recognise and generate effective forms and structures is essential for the arts of divination, ritual and directed vision. Unfortunately (though perhaps understandably), in the past this power has been used to institutionalise magical systems by justifying them in terms of strict cultural or religious biases. It may be that such systems — now largely dated — once had value. By nature, however, they tend to suffocate innovation and stunt growth by fostering false notions of spiritual superiority and promoting unhealthy investment in the system itself.

Nonetheless, despite the potential for misuse, contemporary practitioners of the Magical Way do not ignore or deprecate the intellect, which at its best is an evaluating and clarifying power that is invaluable for keeping our practice and realisations ordered, focused and in perspective.

The intellect enables us to recognise and generate appropriate magical patterns for mediating spiritual power. One of the more enduring and important magical structures is the set of coordinates known as the Seven Directions: Above, Before, Behind, Left, Right and Centre. Each of these has a certain value and significance. Above and Below connect us with the stars and earth; Before and Behind with our journey through life, its potential and our experiences and expectations. Left and Right signify what we accept and reject, or give and take, along the way. The Centre is where all directions merge, end and begin. We all carry this set of magical coordinates around with us, though often not consciously. Most ritual systems, temples, circles and sacred landscapes incorporate this essential pattern of orientation. Through it we relate to forms and flows of sacred space and time

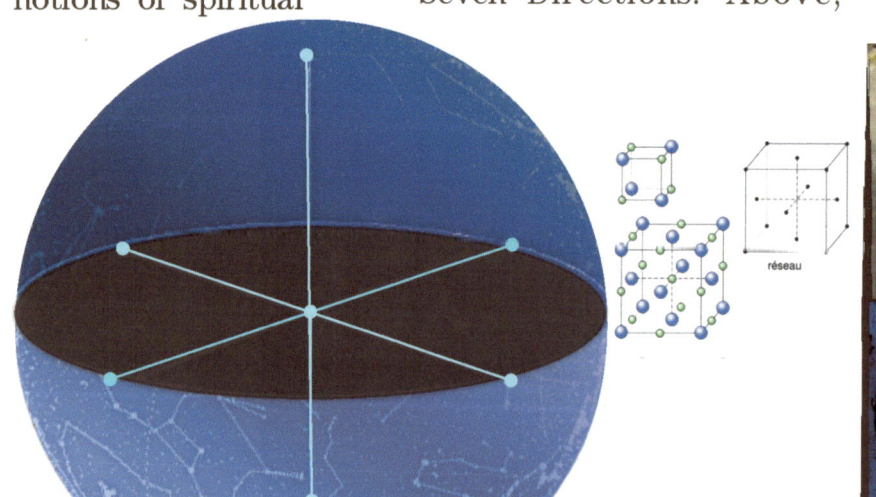

The Seven Directions in a Sphere.

Above: Crystal systems are variations on the sevenfold co-ordinate system of Directions, which defines three dimensional reality as having length, breadth, and height. *Inset*: The inherent structure of a Nautilus shell embodies the essence of the 8th Power in the sense that it conforms to the Fibonacci sequence, which is the basis for much sacred Geometry.

The Seventh Power:

The Power of Emotion, Attraction, Attainment.

The idea of attainment or victory evokes feelings of exaltation, of having reached a peak of personal empowerment. Attainment has to do with passion or emotional motivation. On a personal magical level, attainment results from engaging or riding emotion for the purpose of transformation.

Attainment is closely tied to attraction. There must be something (a goal or grail) that entices us strongly enough that we are motivated to try to attain it. Often in Magic, the goal is the quest itself. The act of striving or seeking embodies its own aim or end.

Emotions are energies generally expressed or released in our relationships with, those around us, with ourselves, and indeed with the world itself. Personal emotional balance aids, empowers and enables wholesome relations with our planet and the world of nature it is home to.

Repressive attempts to contain or bottle up emotion run through much of nineteenth century derived magical training. Such older magical training systems attest a deep-seated fear of emotional power, which has led to its general avoidance and denial. Like nature, emotions are not "rational," and normally function outside or in spite of intellectual frameworks. Thus (like nature) they are often perceived either as insignificant or as threatening and dangerous. But emotive force is deeply connected to authentic Magical Arts. The faculty of engaging or relating is directly linked to one of the most important magical skills — that of empowered participation in inner realms. This is the hidden power of Magic, the power to feel inner realities. Participation of this sort as a power granted to us by our ancestors, who perceived and engaged reality in a more qualitative fashion than most people who are not artists or initiates do today.

The beauty of flowers and mountain peaks both suggest the powers of enchantment and attainment. The journey to the Centre and the journeys to the pinnacle and to beauty are the same Journey taken from different soul-facets or spiritual perspectives.

The Sixth Power:
The Mediating Power, Harmony, Interchanging Radiant Energies, Healing.

Attaining Harmony is an important goal of magical work, whether on individual or collective levels.

The Power of Harmony is the power to reconcile polarities, to be poised in the face of opposition or conflict. It is also about being centred within as a mediator. Harmonising a situation or our selves is not always comfortable or pleasant (though it is empowering) and often involves other Powers, especially the Fourth and Fifth Powers. In other words, it is normally necessary to gain something or let something go in order to achieve Harmony.

Harmony is not something that can be held or controlled with tightness and strain, nor is it the product of giddy pleasantness. Harmony is the dynamic, balanced, expression of growth and development; the poised, rhythmic unfolding of natural energies.

Early on in training, magical practitioners learn to align themselves to the cycles of nature. They are able to attain and maintain personal Harmony by engaging the flowing energies of life — by knowing, accepting and mediating the powers of nature. They allow their life energies to rise and fall, ebb and flow, increase and decrease in tune with the cycles of sun, moon and stars.

One of the duties of being a mediator or practitioner of the Magical Way is to enable transformation by ensuring energy does not become stuck or static. Thus it is sometimes necessary to induce a temporary imbalance to get energies flowing in or toward Harmony. However, deliberate and extreme polarisation of the psyche or of a situation is rarely warranted.

Most often, balance-work – and this applies equally to personal as well as planetary issues– requires the employment of Recovery Magic.[5] Recovery Magic has many forms, from the practice of soul retrieval for personal wholeness or development, to the recovery and release of spiritual patterns and powers latent or captive in human collective memory or in the Earth herself. Such patterns and powers are accessed largely through myth and sacred lore.

Light, specifically Sun, Moon and Starlight are indicative of the powers of Harmony, regeneration and rebirth, which are the essential characteristics of the 6th Power on the Magical Tree. Background Solar light with stars. Above left: Medieval depiction of seasons by Hildegard of Bingen Above Right: Sunset, moon and stars.

The Fifth Power:

The Power that Removes, Catabolic Energy, Taking, Discipline.

The Fifth Power is catabolic. It is the power that removes, takes, dissolves, strips down, or renders essential. It is the great Power that tears away the veils of illusion and removes the false expectations and ideals surrounding much of our awareness and relationships.

In universal terms this is the Power of unending change, of the breaking down of the old to give way to the new. It is a force inherent in the deep earth and the mighty stars. It is a part of the universal cycle of Birth, Death and Regeneration, whether of stars, galaxies, beings, or on lesser levels of seasonal and developmental change. The Fifth Power can seem disruptive and severe, for it ruthlessly clears out stagnant or ossified forms and patterns. However, in this it is really an awakening, liberating energy, a natural force of compensation.

Much responsibility rests with advanced magical practitioners as to how and in what form these catabolic energies are awakened and expressed. Discernment is one of the most important abilities the magical practitioner can cultivate. For without the ability to discern spirits and powers, we are open to errors in judgment and appropriateness that can cause needless suffering to ourselves and others.

The Fifth Power also enables self-discipline, concentration and focus by removing or disabling obstructions and distractions.

Lightning and volcanic fire are natural forces expressing the 5th Power of Taking, for they are destructive forces that essentially and eventually make way for new life — creation through destruction. Creation through destruction is a key principle in Magical training and work.

The Fourth Power:

The Power that Bestows, Anabolic Energy, Giving, Compassion.

The Fifth and Fourth Powers equilibrate each other. Removal, Taking and Discipline counterbalance Bestowal, Giving and Compassion.

Compassion is a word that means to feel or experience together. It is the capacity to recognise ourselves in others and, in that moment of recognition, to realise that at the deepest levels of existence we are all one, unified in the Source.[6] If there were no Source, there could be no Compassion. There is no false, sugary idealism in this. The Power of Compassion has no connection at all to the extremes of limpid sentimentality and blind fanaticism that motivate most do-gooders.

Compassion is such a powerful force because it is a direct expression or affirmation of the Source.

Compassion is not to be confused with pity or sentiment; for pity always involves condescension and assumes superiority. Compassion is neither sentimental nor whiny – it is strong, fierce, powerful, supportive, anabolic or building. It is a positive force. And it is more a cosmic 'universal' force than an emotion, although it finds expression through human emotion. Compassion is the power to give unconditionally, without ulterior motives or hidden agendas.

The existence of Compassion demonstrates the fact that the universe is a holism. Compassion is the great unifying force because it brings everything into relationship with the One. This universal unity is expressed magically through the sign of the equal-armed cross, wherein the junction of axes or arms defines or reveals a central point.

Sovereignty is associated with specific land forms that have legendary or mythological connections to primal Presences or powers of inspiration. *Above: Cadair Idris in Gwynedd, Wales*, "The Seat of Idris", associated with the mythical King and giant Idris who was said to have mastered poetry, astronomy and philosophy.

The Third Power:
Universal Enfolding Power; Inflowing, Enveloping Energies; First Forms.

The Third Power is about sub-stance; the basis of form or the matrix of matter. That both the word matrix and the word matter probably derive from a root meaning mother (ma, mat), emphasises the feminine nature of substance.

Time is a kind of primal form – it contains, limits, enfolds our experience – and thus is an expression of the Third Power. The Inner Realms are timeless. Yet when mortal beings[6] connect with inner realities they are able to bring timeless power into physical expression by letting it flow into temporal forms or rhythms. This mediation of Power into spiralling or cycling time-forms is the secret to regenerating consciousness, as any magical practitioner who has worked with the rhythms of Sacred Time understands.

Human understanding requires merging with particular forms through enfoldment. [7] The key to understanding the Magical Tree is just this: to allow it to enfold you – to merge with it. Typically this is done by visualising the Spheres or Fruits of the Tree fusing with the physical body. Each Sphere expresses or aligns with a bodily (or bio-psychic) centre or node of power and awareness. By engaging the pattern of Spheres and initiating various energy flows in the body, the student is enfolded in the Magical Tree and thus understands it experientially.

A practical magical image of this is enfoldment in the dark cloak of the great Goddess or God. It is an inflowing of power into the darkness of substance, both physical and psychic, even the substance of Being.

Clouds signify the enfolding power that envelops and informs being. *Above*: Stellar clouds envelop the Magical Tree — a metaphor for learning the Tree. *Inset Left:* The Gerum Cloak (ca 2100 BCE), found in a Swedish peat bog in 1920 has markings signifying the starry heavens. and may have been a piece of ancient magical clothing. *Inset Right:* Supercell Thunderclouds in New Mexico seem to enfold the light of the sun.

Second Power:

Universal Outflowing Power, Outgoing Creative Energy, Wisdom.

Like the Third Power, the Second is primarily a universal Power. Only secondarily is it a human quality or characteristic. Wisdom is not simply an attribute of the illumined, experienced or philosophical. It is an active Power in the universe. In esoteric terminology, a wise person is one who taps the unending primordial stream of universal Power, and understands its Truth. Obviously this has little to do with doctrines, dogmas or other religious understandings, for we are dealing with the creative force of Being.

Understanding and Wisdom work hand in hand, as the one enables and activates the other. Through experiencing the primal forms and patterns of the Third Power we gain access to the streams of universal Wisdom of the Second Power. Conversely, Wisdom is continually filtered into magical forms, through which it can be tapped into consciousness.

Because it is connected to truth, Wisdom is often embodied in divine utterance. This is behind the ancient magical perception that the universe was created by the primal shout (usually of laughter or ecstasy) of a divine being. This outpouring of creative force or seed-energy can be identified with the Second Power.

In practical terms The Second Power can be linked to magical utterances, such as vowel calls that are aligned to energy centres along the spinal axis of the human body. This is in resonance of the universal axis or vertical streaming of creative energy that flows through the Three Realms.

Rivers, including the Milky Way or River of Stars, signify the outpouring power that flows through the Structures of perception and reality embodied in the Wheels, Worlds, and Realms *Above*. The Milky Way from Chile.

Powers & Presences

The First Power:

The Source, The Summit, Origination.

The First Power is the Source and originating Energy of the Universe. This is Universal Being in whatever name or under whichever form, whether it be as Creator God or Goddess, or simply pure Light, Brilliance or Universal Energy. The Source is our point of origin as individual consciousness, as a collective or species, as participants in creation.

The Source is both universal wholeness and total potential. In other words, it contains all possible beings and realities. The Source is the ultimate origin of the Real — that which has the greatest value and significance because of its quality of immediacy and realness.

The Source is the summit to which we aspire and grow, and also the root from which we descend. Yet, the Source is no static energy or mere memory, but an organic, living Flow (often imaged in spiral form. See Figure 2e.).

Touching the Source means to bridge personal and even collective modes of being and to enter upon the threshold of the universal. In practical spiritual work, such contact is normally experienced in stages, as spurts or flashes of universal consciousness streaming into the mind.

The whole can be quite unsettling as the Source brings all into being and trues or rights all being that reconnects with it.

The Source has a universal yet totally personal quality, which reflects or refracts into various utterances and forms (of gods, spirits and other divine beings, including the human spirit). This refraction of the Source enables humanity to approach the One through its manifold forms, names and images.

Springs and sparks signify the Source or 1st Power on the Magical Tree.
Above: the Well-spring known as the Pissing Mare, near Lisburn Co. Antrim Northern Ireland *Inset*: Sparks from a blacksmith's forge *Background*: Stars turning round the pole as seen from Bavaria.

The Power of No-Thing:

The Void, the Stillness, the Mystery.

This is not really a Power at all, but non-power, which paradoxically enables all Powers. There is often fear associated with contact with the Void, for it is the Unknown, both pre-creative or potent and post creative or annihilating. Touching the Mystery tends to shatter all false attachments, belief systems, and habitual patterns of behaviour and socialisation.

We may consider the Void as the place or mode of original stillness, the Deep Peace from which Being itself was breathed forth. It is the Great Mystery and the condition of Unknowing, experienced by moving being and awareness beyond perception to pure silence and stillness.

If there is a characteristic of the Void, it is paradox. Thus although the Void is beyond all images, it nonetheless expresses itself in images like Darkness, the Dark Light or Dark Cloud — images that tinge those of the First Power (Infinite Light, Brilliance, Energy, Movement, Wind). The great paradox of the Mystery is that it is the indefinable Source of the Source.

The Divine Void appears in the Mystical teachings and Mythic Cosmologies of both East and West. The Divine Void and the related concepts of Chaos and the Abyss have some resonance with the black hole of Astrophysics *Above*: Artist's representation of a black hole.

Notes to Part I

Page 5

1. The ten-based or decimal system is only one of a number of possible expressions of Universal Being and Energy. Six, Seven and Twelve-based systems are also found in various times and places. But the decimal system fits well with modern thought patterns and perceptions, while containing several of the other significant arrangements. With the addition of the 22 Paths of the Magical Tree, this is realised to an even greater degree.

Page 6

2. Related, and even earlier, is the sevenfold pattern of orientation — the Seven Ways which define Being in terms of the directions of sacred space and time. See the Eighth Power.

3. It is worth noting the works of Gaston Bachelard, arguably one of the twentieth century's most important philosophers of science, yet whose greater contribution lies in his (somewhat difficult) writings on the Four Elements and the poetic imagination. Bachelard recognised that the Elements are not about quantifiable knowledge or information, but about qualitative experience. The Elements imbue material reality with inner meaning.

4. In some magical schools this is called Redemptive Magic, a term that is less useful because, even though the word "redeem" means to recover or release, it carries unfortunate and often narrowly defined theological connotations.

Page 10

5. Obviously, recognising ourselves in others does not always generate Compassion. In fact, nothing is as likely to arouse aversion in us as when we see our shadow side in other's behaviour. In some cases, this kind of self recognition triggers stronger fear-generated responses such as racism, bigotry, injustice and oppression. What distinguishes a compassionate response from a fearful one is that the former affirms and accepts, while the latter denies and rejects.

Page 12

6. That is, beings (humans, animals, plants, insects) who are subject to recognisably finite life cycles. Such cycles, of course, resonate with the cycles of the Sun, Moon, Planets and Stars.

Page 13

7. In Renaissance philosophy, Understanding (intellectus) was perceived as a kind of universal field of consciousness – the realm or modality of archetypal forms. This was linked to the process of learning through contact with a particular spiritual being or god form. For example, visualising and interacting with Hermes was a means of contacting all knowledge with which he was associated. This process of understanding by identification or envelopment was part of the ancient "art of memory." (cf. Francis Yates' ***Art of Memory***)

Practicing the Powers I: Raising the Powers

The following Practices each relate to one of the Powers and to the Deep Peace or Stillness. There is no need to dwell too intensely on each exercise at first, just go through them fairly rapidly to get a feel for the whole sequence. Depending on your experience, needs or goals, you can then focus on each exercise as a specific discipline. Advanced students probably need only a few runs of each practice, less experienced or more dedicated people might spend days or weeks on each individual practice.

This set of practices moves through the Powers from the Tenth to the First and culminates with the Practice of Deep Peace (The Stillness or Void). Each individual practice links with the next, so the whole can also be performed as one practice.

Tenth Power Practice: *Assembling the Elements* (see above, Figure 2a.)

Holding your hands (palms facing toward you) over your

Throat Centre, say "Air;"

Heart Centre, "Fire;"

Sacral Centre "Water;"

Pointing to the earth, say "Earth;"

Sweep your arms out to the side and over your head. Then say "One Being In Light." (void is most obvious in pause between breaths)

Ninth Power Practice: *The Arousal.*

Pointing to the earth say "Light becomes Earth;" Feel light and power rising from the deeps of the planet into your hands and feet.

Raise your arms to the side and over your head in six steps as follows:

Your hands are level with your genitals, say "Earth becomes Water;"

Level with your heart, say "Water becomes Fire;"

Level with your Throat, say "Fire become Air;"

Arms over your head, say "Air becomes Light;"

Bring arms down in arcs to either side (describing a circle) until hands meet pointing down in front of you, say "Being One In Light;"

Cross arms over on chest, say. "One Being In Light."

As you do this practice feel light and power rising up from the earth through your feet, and into your body in stages to the levels marked by your hands, as indicated in steps i) to iv).

Eighth Power Practice: *The Compass*

As you do this Practice, be aware of power flowing in from each direction.

Stand facing North, raise arms over head, say "Beginning;"

Lower arms to sides, pointing to earth, say "Becoming;"

Turn to East, cross arms over chest, say "Arising"

Turn to South, say "Sustaining;"

Turn to West, say "Descending;"

Turn to North, say "Returning."

Seventh Power Practice: *Opening the Centre:* Facing North, arms crossed over chest, say "From Returning Light the Centre is Born" Uncross arms. Be aware of a point of light appearing in your heart. Feel its power grow as it expands to a sphere that encompasses you.

Sixth Power Practice: *Harmony:* Attune yourself inwardly to the harmony of the diurnal and seasonal rhythms (which correlate to the initiatory cycles of Birth, Sovereignty, Sacrifice and Rebirth).

The following are merely introductory suggestions for each season, you can and should develop the visions more fully and completely (Similar cycles can also be developed based on the rhythms of moon and stars).

Face East— See and feel a spring scene at dawn. The Sun rises as shoots grow and small flower buds open. Birds sing, animals stir, tend their young, and so on.

Face South— The summer sun shines high in the sky. Flowers are in full bloom, trees in full leaf, creatures are fully grown and in their prime.

Face West— The Sun is setting, autumn leaves are falling, fruits are ripened and seeds are bursting from flowers and grain. Creatures, mature and seasoned, seek places to shelter from the coming winter or prepare to die in harmony with the rhythms of nature.

Face North— The sky is dark and starlit. The Trees are leafless, the ground stark and bare. Few creatures are about, for now is the time of sleep and regenerating energy in preparation for the rebirth of the cycles of the day and seasons.

Fifth Power Practice. *Creation through Destruction:* A common ritual action involving the Fifth Power is to strike a match, which is the explosive creation of a universe in miniature. This deceptively simple act of creation through destruction is an important preparation for all magical work. It constitutes a clearing and preparation of sacred space before lighting the central flame around which the ritual energies will circulate. A simple utterance, such as "Light out of Darkness," is useful when striking your match (which should ideally be a wooden match struck on a sacred stone). Once struck the match should be placed in a bowl of earth and allowed to burn itself out.

Fourth Power Practice: *The Giver of Light:* This consists of nothing more than lighting a candle, as a magical gesture resonant with the idea of providing a guiding or stable spiritual light. As you light the flame, be aware that you are raying out compassion to the four quarters of East, West, South and North.

Third Power Practice: *Enfolding:* This is the extinguishing of a candle, the enfolding of the powers of light into the forms of time and space, which are carried with you into the outer world. Enfolding is an important part of any magical ritual practice. Feel the essential power of your magical work come upon you like a cloak as the physical light goes out.

Second Power Practice: Uttering

Utter the Vowel Call **A-E-I-U-O.**

Centre, A,(pronounced soft like "Ah") = Being or Spirit East, I (long, like "eye") = Fire, South, U (long, like OO) = Water, West, O (long, like "Oh")= Earth, North.

This vocalisation, independent of any particular tradition, is a way of expressing the flow and rhythms of creative energy in the universe. In a ritual context, such utterances open up channels of wisdom and creative power that set the tone and primary inner directive of the work.

First Power Practice: *Spiralling:* Simply walk a spiral. For the present, do this from circumference to centre, which is a following of spiritual power to the Source. As you reach centre, feel your self dissolve in a sea of brilliance.

Non Power Practice: *Entering the Deep Peace:* Breathe regularly. Be aware that the rhythm of your breathing tunes and harmonises your entire being.

Allow Deep Peace or stillness to penetrate your being. Still your physical body: your tensions dissipate, your muscles relax, your heartbeat slows, and all the internal processes of your body harmonise. Still your desires and emotions, allowing them to become quiescent and harmonised to the great flow of Being. Now let your thoughts too become still. Concentrate only upon your breathing. Empty yourself of all else. There is only the breathing, the rhythm of the Deep Peace.

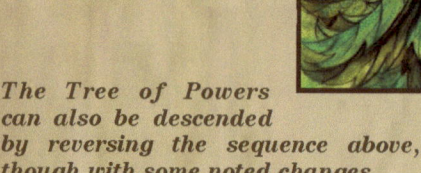

Practicing the Powers II: Descending the Powers

The Tree of Powers can also be descended by reversing the sequence above, though with some noted changes.

0 Non Power Practice: as above,

1 Spiralling: as above but from centre to circumference, feeling your self coming into being out of brilliance.

2 Uttering: as above

3 Enfolding: Form your forefingers and thumbs into a triangle. Hold apex up before your throat (Air), then heart (Fire) centres, then apex down before genital (Water) centre, and a little lower, towards the ground (Earth centre). This is an enfolding of the Utterance into form.

4 Face front, right, behind and left in turn, stopping briefly at each direction. At each pause, touch your left hand to your heart and sweep it out before you as you send compassion out to all beings in that quarter.

5 as above

6 as above.

7 as above, but start with, arms uncrossed, say "From Returning Light the Centre is Born" then cross arms.

8-10 as above.

Part II: *Enlivening The Magical Tree— The Mystery & The Ten Presences.*

An important aspect of the Magical Tree is the idea of Spiritual Presences. This is because the Tree is a Living Tree and thus expresses being as well as power. Indeed, Presences are the way mortal beings are able to relate to the Powers. The keyword here is relate, for it's all about building relationships with spiritual realities. Relationships are what allow power to flow between beings and the realms or worlds they are centred in. In the past, Presences have been given a specific sectarian or traditional context, which is fine for those working solely within such a context. However, the Magical Tree is a universal form, and needs to be understood also from a universal standpoint.

In the late nineteenth and through the twentieth century, some magicians began to realise this and made attempts to relate various pantheons, god aspects or god-forms to the Spheres of the Tree. These attempts failed, however, because in most cases the understanding of Spiritual Presences was as immature as the approach to the Tree was flawed. The Magical Tree was generally viewed as a "filing system" (in today's parlance, a "primitive computer") and the various presences — whether these were imaged as god-forms, archangels, or other spiritual beings — were treated mostly as units, attributions, or data to be labeled and stuffed into little pigeon hole versions of the Spheres. Underlying this there was usually either a sense of monotheistic religious and academic superiority, which reduced individual spiritual beings to little more than the dim glimmerings of unevolved peoples, or there was simple ignorance regarding the nature of spiritual presences.

Now while it is true that many spiritual beings resonate — it is a serious error to treat them as identical. Yet even today many magicians perpetuate this error by indiscriminately identifying the deities of various pantheons, reducing them to little more than placard-like, cartoonish aliases of one another, or sometimes mere, psychological "archetypes". A similar error is carried forward in much of the modern esoteric approach to Astrology, which has had its own enduring and unhealthy effect on the Magical Tree tradition.*

Presences are the way mortal beings are able to relate to The Powers. The keyword here is "relate", for it's all about building relationships with spiritual realities. Relationships are what allow power to flow between beings and the realms or worlds they are centred in. I suggest reading the entire folio through at least once before trying any of the practices. Primal Presences are universal all-encompassing emanations of Powers. Primal Presences emanate into Personal and transpersonal modalities embodied in what are generally thought of as Spiritual beings

What I offer here is in no sense theological or sectarian. It is entirely practical— a way of approaching spiritual beings in a universal way, yet one that will also work for any specific tradition. The approach is holistic and organic rather than systematic, a flexible set of guidelines for understanding and making contact with Living Sacred Presences.

---

* This is not to suggest that there are no Astrologers today who understand the Deeper issues of Star Lore and Astro-cycles

Powers & Presences

0 & 1 The Mystery & The Source

All presences and powers flow from the Void, the Unknown, the Mystery. The Primal Presences are the faces of the Void and the first of these is called the Source. The Source is like the living dream of the Primal Sleeper, generating reality.

The Source may be encountered in a mighty vision, found in the waters of a quiet spring, sensed within a seed, a flame, or discovered at the start of any enterprise. This is the presence of origination, here at the beginning of all things.

In world religions, the Source is remembered in the myths of the *deus otiosus*, the withdrawn deity. This is because religious traditions tend to stasis, to a status quo, and the living originating Presence withdraws as the tradition becomes increasingly fixed and rigid.

The Source is most often imaged as a Divine Creator or Creatrix who stands at the beginning of all Being. The primordial Reality that generates everything that is. Even the Great Dreamer at the beginning and end of time, whose dreaming mediates all into being through time, space and event.

Powers & Presences

2 The High One, The Utterer.

This Presence is encountered in the hills, mountains, and all high places of the world. The High One is also met in streams and rivers, the risen sun, moon, stars, the Milky Way and in the weather and atmosphere. In sacred lore and in inner spiritual work the Presence of the High One usually appears in the beings of the OverRealm: giants, goddesses, gods, angels and heroic figures of the sky and stars. In monotheistic religious traditions this is God The Transcendent, "The Word." Because this is the presence of Flow, it is often imaged as River deities or streams of beings. The streams of being are named variously as the White and Red dragons, rivers of tears and Blood, or the Bright and Shadow Streams of Being.* Bright and Shadow is determined by the relational flow of the stream: Forwards and upwards flows the Bright Stream in relation to one's conscious awareness, while Backwards and downwards flows the dark shadow stream of being.

* For more on the Streams of Being, see my book *The Mystery of the Seven Directions*, especially Chapter 11

The Outflowing and Inflowing of the Stream of Being is well-illustrated in this painting by William Blake. The stream is flowing in one direction, while the beings within it face the opposite direction giving the sense that the current could reverse at any time. This rhythm or pulsing is known in esoteric (Qabalistic) Lore as Run and Return.

Powers & Presences

3 The Deep One, The Enfolder

The Presence of the Deep is found in valleys, caves, hollows, forests, pools, lakes, seas, etc. The Deep one is also met in all that is below the horizon, including (at appropriate times) the planets, stars, sun and moon. In spiritual practice and sacred lore, the Deep Presence is met in the beings of the UnderRealm: deities of shadow, fire, and the inner light, titans, watchers or sleepers (who may be gods, goddesses, heroes, saints or priests and priestesses), in certain kinds of faery beings, and in the ancestors. The Enfolder is the great presence that teaches through experience. The Deep One enables us to learn by merging with a particular structure or stream. This can feel like a coiling of energy about one, an embracing presence that imparts understanding through resonance and symbiosis.

The Deep One is a great presence that encoils and enfolds our consciousness enabling understanding and experience on a deep root level. Often this presence appears in the form of dreams and Dreamers or simply as a cascade of consciosness that immerses one in a particular form of awareness.

4 *The Sovereign, Benefactor or Giving Presence*

This is the Presence met with in every moment of increase, of bounty, of the coming forth of life, as in the opening of flowers, the ripening of fruit, the birth and growth of mortal beings. The Giving Presence is also found in the building of sacred structures and temples.

In inner work and sacred lore the Giver is met in goddesses of birth, in sacred vessels of plenty (like the cornucopia, cauldron of plenty, and the grail), in sovereignty and sovereign deities, in weaving deities, culture heroes and way showers, flower maidens and so on.

The Benefactor also called the Great Giver, often imaged as a nurturing Mother Goddess or a beneficent father God. The Bestowing Presence is closely connected to the Power of Sovereignty, particularly as it relates one's own Sovereign awareness and self rule. Yhis Presence bestows individuality and control over one's own life energies and the forms or manifestations that radiate from them.

Powers & Presences

5 The Warrior or Taking Presence

This is the Presence that breaks down, removes, unravels. Whenever we encounter loss, decline, death, destruction, there we may meet the Presence of the Taker.

The Taker tests and tries by ruthlessly removing all false attachments and beliefs and exposes all behaviour unconditionally to the power of divine justice.

In sacred lore and esoteric working, this Presence is met in the Great Guardian beings, the destroyers, the slayers, and Battle deities, in the judging and binding deities, and in sentinels, for this is also the presence involved in protecting the innocent, the guileless and the harmless.

The Warrior or The Taker is the presence that burns away of illusions and false notions of self. *Above*: William Blake's Los (Urthona), the fearsome Blacksmith, who tempers Spirit in his forge of creative fire Los is Sol in reverse, and thus the Light of the UnderRealm. *Inset*: Enitharma, a Hecate-like figure in Blake's Mythology, the female emanation of Los.

Powers & Presences

6 The Radiant One

The Radiant One is the primal presence of beauty, centrality, of mediation and equilibrium. It is the saving and liberating presence, which appears in sacred lore and esoteric work as beings (saviours, divine children, innocents, sacred sovereigns, sacrificial gods & goddesses) and in harmonising situations and events. The Radiant Presence unconditionally mediates spiritual energy, keeping things in balance though the constant interplay of complementary energies.

We can meet the Radiant One in moments of harmony, beauty, and appreciation,

But also in times of personal sacrifice and healing.

The centring, harmonising Presence of the Radiant One wakens and enlightens consciousness into wholeness., though it bears always the danger of inflation. *Background:* Lucifer, Light Bearer. *Inset right:* The Man of Light rises from the UnderRealm.

7 The Lover

The Sacred Primal Presence of the Lover evokes energy similar to the passion that is aroused in a love affair. Just so things are clear, this generally has little to do with engaging in "astral sex" or with masturbation in connection with inner spiritual contacts (but of course there could be this, in which case the contact becomes more complicated and risks being sullied by getting entangled with personal issues of adequacy, maturity, and morality). The awe-inspiring presence of the Lover will evoke and often enable a dramatic change in life direction. This is an awakening and upraising presence and is, with Illuminator and Upholder, one of the triad of presences of arousal.

The Lover presence expresses or instigates strong feelings of attraction to something or someone. In Lore and spiritual work and experience, the Lover is often met in beings associated with eroticism, sexuality and ecstasy. These include deities of fertility and fecundity, spiritual beings in myth and legend who have sexual encounters with mortals, and the erotic mysticism of certain saints. The Lover presence is also tied to ancestral lines. We see the Lover manifest in the notions of the Fetch or Faery Other, the latter often involves connections with animals and Nature in general.

The Presence of The Lover stimulates awakening through attraction and arousal. One's personal Quest and purpose are often activated and evoked by this Presence.

Powers & Presences

8 The Knower, The Mentor, The Smith.

This Presence expresses itself through the figures of spiritual teachers, mentors and tutors, bards, poets artists, awakeners, initiators and mediators. Also this presence is found in magical temples and traditions, which embody and express patterns of illumination and initiation. The Knower is deeply linked to the raising or arousal of the inner light or fire and is one of the great Arousing Presences.

This is the the shining one who initiates through illumination. This Presence complements that of the Lover and is likewise somewhat concerned with the awakening effects of sexual energy.

The collage of images above shows various ways in which William blage imaged, and hence mediated, the Presence of the Knower. *Top Right:* skillfill worker of knowledge patterns; *Bottom Right* : Bard, *Bottom left:* Crafter/Smith

Powers & Presences

9 The Weaver/Upholder

This is the Primal Presence that stirs the foundational energies and arouses the psychic centres in the human body. On a deeper level it is the flow or arousal of primal energies in the planet, the deep earth power or dragon force that is mirrored and inextricably interlinked with human sexual and spiritual energy.

This is not a sexual presence in terms of polarity or compensation, it is a whole power in and of itself though it is often embodied by the image or incarnation of dual dragons, serpents, or spiritual fires.

Polar forces are, however, activated by this presence, for as the power rises it passes across certain threshold patterns that trigger energies that attract or draw (us across) opposites into tension, maintaining, sustaining, or upholding a set of universal energy patterns or cosmic psychic structures. The aim of the magical arousal of sexual energy (Ninth Power) and subsequent polarity exchange (Seventh and Eight Powers) is to partly to assist and enable partners to achieve wholeness. However, there is a deeper significance here associated with increased levels of mediation and spiritual service — in other words it's about true partnership, not about promoting relationships that are dependent and artificial.

William Blake's Vision images several forms of a great UnderRealm Presence as Weaver, Blacksmith and Lightbearer. These appear in connection with the ancient megalithic temples that Blake associated with the Dragon Force.

Powers & Presences

10 The Illuminated Landscape, The Dreamer

This is where Primal Presence expresses itself in physical terms through landscapes, forests, mountains, seas and rivers. and through the Elements, often connected to the great Dreamers who generate Sacred Landscapes around the globe.

This Presence has much similarity to the power of *Mana* among the Polynesians, the *Orenda* of the Iroquois, *Pneuma* of the Greeks, the Lakota *Wakan*, the Hebraic *Shekinah* etc. This is a permeating magical power, present in all sacred objects events and beings.

This presence centralises itself in figures from myth and spiritual tradition such as the Chinese Pangu, Norse Ymir, the Iroquois Star Woman, Lucifer and Christ, and Adam and Eve of the *Cave of Treasures* traditions.

Indeed, all divine beings who interact with the earth, sea, sky or elements are emanations of this Presence.

Background: The Primal Couple Lighted in the Land and overshone by the Radiant One,

Relational Polarity and The Presences

An important characteristic of the Primal Presences on the Magical tree is that they can appear (emanate) as either male or female. The apparent gender of any given Presence is **Relational** in the sense it depends on the *polarity* of other Presences. For instance, The Presence of Sphere 4, The Sovereign, emanates as either male or female, but whichever it is, the obverse Presence in Sphere 5, The Warrior, will appear of the opposite gender.* The Harmonic Presences will be of the same polarity, The High One (2.) and the Lover (7.), while the complementary Presences, the Deep One (3.) and The Knower (4.), are opposite in gender to the Sovereign.

* As in the case of the Irish Dagda and the Morrigan, the Greek Zeus and Athena, or the Egyptian Isis and Horus.

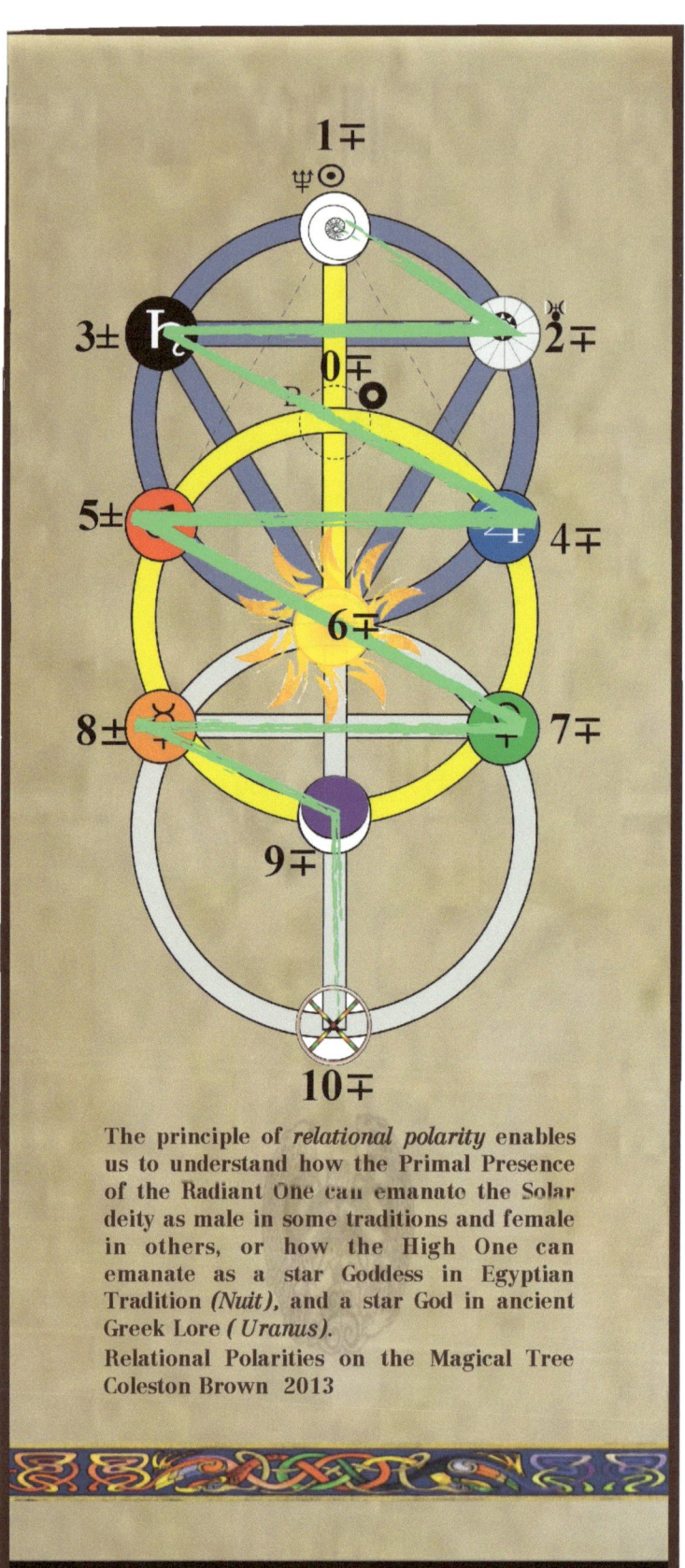

The principle of *relational polarity* enables us to understand how the Primal Presence of the Radiant One can emanate the Solar deity as male in some traditions and female in others, or how the High One can emanate as a star Goddess in Egyptian Tradition *(Nuit)*, and a star God in ancient Greek Lore *(Uranus)*.

Relational Polarities on the Magical Tree
Coleston Brown 2013

Working with Presences:

Relational considerations also come into play when we work with Presences. First and foremost is the realisation that contacts with OtherWorld Presences are relationships and as such require the same work and effort as do our outer world relationships. In the Practices below Presences can be either specific ones deliberately called forth or they may be encountered spontaneously.

Practicing the Presences I The Empty Chair:

Sit in your own chair with an empty chair before you.

Enter the Deep Peace (see above page 20)

Set a Centre by lighting a candle, some incense or by setting out a stone or filling a bowl of water.

Be aware of a presence emerging from the Centre, circling to the right, behind you passing to your left and to the front.

The presence sits in the empty chair opposite you.

Commune with the presence, being particularly aware of any impressions, sensations, thoughts, feelings, etc., that may arise.

Acknowledge the presence, by raising your hand or nodding

Then be aware of the connection fading and record your experience

Practicing the Presences II The Wheel of Presences:

Proceed as above (i-iv), but with no empty chair.

Presences emerge from the centre and form a circle around you.

Be aware of streams of energy and connection between you and the Presences and among the Presences themselves.

Commune and Close as above (v-vii).

Presences and The Three Wheels

Presences can also be worked with effectively when aligned with the Three wheels of the Tree:

a) Stellar-centred Presences:

Source, High One, Deep One, Giver, Taker, Radiant One, Mystery

b) Solar-centred Presences:

Mystery, Sovereign, Lover, Knower, Warrior, Radiant One.

c) Lunar-centred Presences

Radiant One, Lover, Knower, Dreamer, Weaver.

Primal Presences may emanate as personal or transpersonal contacts.

Personal contacts are related to on a day-to-day, often informal, basis.

Transpersonal contacts are usually connected to cosmic rhythms and cycles of change. Included here emanate figures such as Archangels, gods, deities, great transforming and mediating Beings. More on the nature of Presences will be found in my Forthcoming Folio *The Communion of Presences* (due September 2013)

About The Author

Coleston Brown enjoys a simple life in the Irish countryside. He spends most of his free time quietly working on various projects designed to further the Faery-Human Covenant and the Magical Way.

www.magicalways.com

Picture Credits

Pages 4-36, Celtic Knot page runner © 1997 by Jessie Skillen.

Page 1: The Magical Tree © Coleston Brown 2013

Page 5

The Magical Tree with Lightning Zag. © Coleston Brown 2013

Page 6
The Four Elements centred on Spirit. © Coleston Brown 2013

Page 7

Volga River Delta. Image source: NASA Public Domain.

Inset: the Venus of Laussel. Image courtesy of Musée d'Aquitaine à Bordeaux, licensed under the Creative Commons Attribution 3.0 Unported license.

Page 8

Right: The Seven Directions in a Sphere © Coleston Brown 2013

middle: Cubic crystal lattice. Image credit: Christophe Dang Ngoc Chan. Licensed under the Creative Commons Attribution 3.0 Unported license.

Right: Cubic crystal. Image credit: Rob Lavinsky. Licensed under the Creative Commons Attribution 3.0 Unported license.

Inset: Nautilus Shell. Image credit: Chris 73. Licensed under the Creative Commons Attribution 3.0 Unported license.

Page 9

The Matterhorn by Edward Theodore Compton, 1879 Image in the Public Domain

Inset: Alpine flower. Image Credit: Vyacheslav Argenberg Licensed under the Creative Commons attribution 2.0 Generic license.

Page 10

Background: Picture by Charles. Image in the Public Domain.

Left: Hildegard of Bingen. Image in the Public Domain.

Right: Image Credit: Jon Sullivan Image in the Public Domain.

Page 11

Lightning over a volcano. Image Credit: Oliver Spalt. Licensed under the Creative Commons Attribution 3.0 Unported license.

Page 12:

Cadair Idris in Gwynedd, Wales. Image credit: Travellor100. Licensed under the Creative Commons Attribution 3.0 Unported license.

Page 13

Stellar Clouds. Image credit NASA. Image in the Public Domain

Page 14:

Milky Way Arch. Image Credit: ESO. Licensed under the Creative Commons Attribution 3.0 Unported license.

Page 15

The Well-spring known as the Pissing Mare, near Lisburn, Co. Antrim Northern Ireland   © 2012 by Jessie Skillen.

Inset: Sparks from a blacksmith's forge. image credit Tobias R, Metoc. Licensed under the Creative Commons Attribution-Share Alike 2.5 Generic license.

Background: Stars turning round the pole as seen from Bavaria. Image credit: Udo Kügel. Licensed under the Creative Commons Attribution 3.0 Unported license.

Page 16

Artist's representation of a black hole. Image credit: NASA. Image in the Public Domain

Page 20

Green Man half face © 1994 by Jessie Skillen.

Pages 22-31

Pictures by William Blake 1757-1827. Images in the Public Domain.

Page 32

Relational Polarities on the Magical Tree © Coleston Brown 2013.